THE LAO TZU

Written by Lao Zi
Translated with an introduction by
An Yu

Published by Asian Culture Press
1942 Broadway St., Suite 314c,
Boulder, CO 80302, United States
Web: www.asianculture.press

Published in the United States of America

First paperback edition May 2022
本书2022年5月在美国第一次出版

FOREWORD

The Lao Tzu was authored by Lao Zi (about 571-471 BC), who served as the librarian in the royal library during the Zhou Dynasty. He was an ancient Chinese intellectual, philosopher, and advocate for change.

In China, The Lao Tzu (in honor of Lao Zi) is also known as *Tao Te Ching* or *Dao De Jing* (道德经). "Tao" (道) is pronounced as "Dao" in Chinese, "Te"(德通得) means achievement and is pronounced as "De," and "Ching" (经) means scripture and is pronounced as "Jing." The Tao Te Ching is considered the scripture of achieving harmony with the Tao.

There are a lot of versions of translation of the Tao Te Ching in the world, and why did I spend more than 10 years translating it again?

The Zhou Dynasty was an era under rule by man, and the rulers were corrupted and acted arbitrarily. Hence, King Jing of Zhou decided to promulgate the Tao Te Ching as a new belief throughout the country to carry out reforms in 522 BC. Unfortunately, King Jing of Zhou died young, and after his death, his ministers staged a coup to abolish the reforms.-Wang Zhenjin(a Chinese freelance researcher).

I

Thus, my decision to embark on the journey of creating my very own translation of this body of work was unavoidable and not taken lightly. It stemmed from a deep reverence for the wisdom contained within and a desire to unveil its true meaning for modern readers. Having acquainted myself with various translations made by others, I found that many failed to convey the true essence of these texts.

In undertaking the task of translating the Tao Te Ching, my aim is to present its timeless wisdom in a manner that resonates with contemporary Western readers while remaining faithful to its original Chinese meaning.

I firmly believe that by reconnecting with the profound teachings of the Tao Te Ching, we can gain invaluable insights into navigating the complexities of our modern world.

It is my hope that this translation of the Tao Te Ching will serve as a beacon of wisdom and inspiration for all who seek to embark on a journey of self-discovery and enlightenment through Chinese philosophy and literature.

With reverence and gratitude,
An Yu

About the Tao

The Tao remains unseen and its name unknown, leaving its gender undetermined. However, all the past, present, and future originate from the Tao.Therefore, Lao Zi had to refer to the Tao as the Mother of all, as Providence and Fortune; he had to designate the Tao as She, Her, and One; he had to give the name Tao to Her.

Why is the Tao considered the Mother of all? It's because the Tao gives rise to non-being and being; these two give rise to the sky, the earth, and humankind; and these three give rise to everything.

The Tao is immortal and everlasting, for She is impartial, just, and selfless to all. The Tao is eternal, hence impartiality, justice, and selflessness endure eternally. Therefore, if we seek eternity, we should follow the Tao.

The Tao is mainly described in Chapters 1, 4, 6, 14, 21, 25, 32, 34, 35, 40, 41, 42, and 51.

Contents

Chapter 1

1 If the Tao can be defined, this one is not the eternal Tao;

2 If the Tao can be named, this name is not the eternal name of the Tao.

3 Non-being is the beginning of the sky and the earth;

4 Being is the root of all.

5 Therefore, always from non-being, try to find the mystery of the Tao;

6 Always from being, try to find the boundary of the Tao.

7 Non-being and being, with different names and both from the Tao, are called mystery and abstruseness.

8 The Tao, extremely mysterious and abstruse, is the origin of all wonders.

(The law of the Tao: all is the cycle from non-being to being and to non-being again.)

Chapter 2

1 When know what good is, know what evil is;

2 When know what unconditional help is, know what conditional help is.

3 Therefore, being and non-being are relative, so are difficult and easy, so are long and short, so are high and low, so are tune and sound, and so are front and back.

4 Therefore, a Tao follower does not act and impose orders arbitrarily:

5 When things rise, he or she does not disturb them;

6 When things appear, he or she does not control them;

7 When things develop, he or she does not depend on them;

8 When things succeed, he or she does not claim credit for it.

9 Because he or she does not take credit, his or her credit is lasting.

Chapter 3

1 Do not select sages, so people will not scramble for fame and wealth;
2 Do not value rare treasures, so people will not become robbers;
3 Do not propagate what arouses desire, so people will not get upset.
4 Therefore, a Tao follower's principles to administer a nation are:
5 Empty people' s pride, yet fill their belly;
6 Weaken people' s desire, yet sturdy their body.
7 Always let them free from trickery and greed, and let the wicked have no audacity to act arbitrarily.
8 Whoever does not act arbitrarily will not fail.

Chapter 4

1 The Tao is transparent and shapeless, yet the Tao's effect never ever ends.
2 The Tao, mysterious and abstruse, is the master of all;
3 The Tao is invisible yet real.
4 I do not know where the Tao came from, but I just know that it existed before the universe.

Chapter 5

1 The sky and the earth impartially treat everything;
2 A Tao follower impartially treats every person.
3 Are not the sky and the earth like a pair of bellows?
4 The middle of it is empty, but air comes out endlessly when it works.
5 Acting arbitrarily incurs failure, so it is better to keep righteous.

Chapter 6

1 The Tao is called a mysterious Mother;
2 The mysterious Mother is called the origin of the sky and the earth.
3 The Tao is shapeless yet real, and Her effect never ever ceases.

Chapter 7

1 The sky and the earth can exist for a long time;
2 They can do so, for they do not exist for themselves.
3 Thus, they can live for a long time.
4 Therefore, although a Tao follower puts his or her own interests last, his or her interests are the first to be realized;
5 Although he or she is regardless of his or her own interests, his or her interests are saved from damage.
6 Is it not for his or her selflessness?
7 So, he or she succeeds in achieving his or her own interests.

Chapter 8

1 Whoever helps others unconditionally is like water:

2 Water is good at nourishing things, but does not scramble for benefit from them, and gathers in the lower place that people dislike, so water approximates the Tao;

3 Whoever helps others unconditionally is good at adapting to new situations, staying calm, sharing with others, endeavoring his or her best, and seizing the moment.

4 Because he or she does not scramble for fame and wealth from others, he or she is not hated.

Chapter 9

1 It is better to stop feeling complacent
  soon;
2 Nothing can always stay sharp;
3 Nobody can guard wealth forever;
4 Pride and luxury incur disaster;
5 Keeping a low profile after winning a
  tremendous success accords with the Tao.

Chapter 10

1 Can anybody, a soulful follower, never betray the Tao?
2 Can anybody always stay temperate like a newborn baby?
3 Can anybody completely clean up their desire-filled mind and return to purity?
4 Can anybody always rule a state by law for the people?
5 Can anybody always get calm when temptations appear?
6 Can anybody intelligent enough always keep honest?

Chapter 11

1 For there is the round hole of emptiness
   in the centre of a cart wheel, where thirty
   spokes radiate, the wheel is of use;
2 For there is the volume of emptiness in a
   container made of clay, the container is
   of use;
3 For there is the rooms of emptiness in a
   house, so the house is of use;
4 Therefore, it is for the emptiness that
   they are of use.

Chapter 12

1 Looking at colorful objects too much blinds the eye;
2 Listening to music too much deafens the ear;
3 Tasting flavored food too much damages the tongue.
4 Desire makes people crazy;
5 Rare treasures make people evil.
6 Therefore, a Tao follower only demands for getting well fed and clothed, but does not wallow in worldly desires.
7 So,do not indulge in worldly desires, yet stay content with getting well fed and clothed.

Chapter 13

1 Getting adulated and getting snubbed
  make people uneasy;
2 Treat the awareness of lurking perils with
  the same importance like life itself.
3 Why do getting adulated and getting
  snubbed make people uneasy?
4 Getting adulated is not good, but people
  are surprised if they get adulated, and
  worried if they get snubbed.
5 So, getting adulated and getting snubbed
  make people uneasy.
6 Why Treat the awareness of lurking
  perils with the same importance as life
  itself?
7 I can find lurking perils because I
  treasure my life;
8 If I do not treasure my life, I have no
  lurking perils!
9 So, a nation can be entrusted to whoever
  treats the awareness of lurking perils with
  the same importance as life itself;
10 A nation can be taken over by whoever
  treats it with the same importance as
  valuing life itself.

Chapter 14

1 The Tao is invisible, inaudible and intangible.
2 These characteristics can not be identified.
3 So She is whole of invisibility, inaudibility and intangibility.
4 Her top is not bright, and Her bottom is not dark;
5 She is infinite and omnipresent.
6 This is called as the shape of no shape and image of no image, which is called as indefinite.
7 In front of Her, can not find Her head;
8 Behind Her, can not find Her back.
9 Adherence to the Tao existing since time immemorial can deal with all present;
10 When understand the beginning of all, understand the law of the Tao.

Chapter 15

1 Ancient Tao followers were keen and unfathomable.
2 Because they were unfathomable, I have to reluctantly describe them:
3 Careful like wading through the frozen stream in winter;
4 Cautious like keeping guard against the threats from all around;
5 Solemn like the guest visiting a strange place;
6 Vivid like the melting brook in spring;
7 Pure like the uncut log;
8 Modest like the bottomless gorge;
9 Impartial like the river never rejecting small rivulets;
10 Calm like the limitless ocean;
11 Resolute like the endless strong winds.
12 How to make muddy water clear?
13 Stop disturbing it, and then it clears slowly.
14 How to make stability lasting?
15 Reform step by step, and then stability can last for long.
16 Whoever grasps the truth does not feel complacent;
17 Whoever is not complacent can progress at all times.

Chapter 16

1 Stay completely modest and calm;
2 When things appear, I observe the cycle of them:
3 They are numerous and diverse, and finally return to non-being respectively.
4 Returning to non-being means the completion of the cycle and eternal tranquility;
5 The cycle is the law of the Tao, and whoever knows the everlasting law is wise.
6 Whoever does not know it will act arbitrarily and do dangerous things.
7 Whoever knows the everlasting law is impartial;
8 Whoever is impartial is righteous;
9 Whoever is righteous can govern a state;
10 Whoever can govern a state obeys Providence;
11 Whoever obeys Providence obeys the Tao;
12 Whoever obeys the Tao is safe for the whole life.

(The law of the Tao: all is the cycle from non-being to being and to non-being again.)

Chapter 17

1 A good monarch is imperceptible to people;
2 A bad monarch is adulated by others;
3 A worse monarch is dreaded by others;
4 The worst monarch is vilified by others.
5 If a monarch does not keep promise, people will not believe him or her naturally.
6 A good monarch does not impose orders arbitrarily;
7 After achieving success, people all say, "That is how it should be."

Chapter 18

1 When the Tao is neglected, partiality and faction will arise;

2 When a state is under rule by man, fraud and trick will be widespread.

3 In the case of family disharmony, obedient sons are chosen as a social model;

4 In a corrupt state, loyal ministers are selected as a national model .

Chapter 19

1 When sage-selecting and rule by man are abandoned, people will benefit immensely;

2 When partiality and faction are abandoned, people will love and respect each other;

3 When speculation and scrambling for profit from people are abandoned, nowhere will thieves arise.

4 Governing a nation solely by the three principles above is not enough.

5 So, let people have a spiritual shelter, let them be pure and modest, let them have no selfish ideas, and let them be free from mental disturbance by not pursuing worldly desires.

Chapter 20

1 How different is answer from rebuke?
2 How distinct is good from evil?
3 Fear what others fear;
4 When will this blind following that has existed since ancient times come to end?
5 Others are very jubilant, like attending a banquet and ascending a height for a distant view in spring;
6 It is only I who am calm, unconcerned like a newborn baby unable to laugh yet, and confused like a person losing his or her way home.
7 Others feel very successful, while it is only I who feel very defeated.
8 How stupid my heart is!
9 Others are so shrewd, while it is only I who am so puzzled;
10 Others are so sharp, while it is only I who am so blunt.
11 Others consider themselves as great and uncommon, while it is only I who consider myself as tiny and ordinary;
12 It is only I who, different from others, respect and follow the Tao.

Chapter 21

1 The greatest success comes from the Tao.
2 The Tao is elusive and indeterminate:
3 Her form is shrouded in obscurity, Her presence in uncertainty, Her spirit in profoundness;
4 Her spirit is very real and exact.
5 From ancient times to the present, Her name never ever disappeared, and the origin of all can be known according to Her.
6 How do I know the origin of all?
7 Follow the Tao.

Chapter 22

1 Whoever makes compromise can reach agreement;

2 Whoever is tolerant can achieve it;

3 Whoever remains modest can become full;

4 Whoever discards old practices can make progress;

5 Whoever takes less can gain more;

6 Whoever is greedy for too much can get confused.

7 Therefore, a Tao follower reveres the Tao as the example of a country:

8 Not showy, thus wise;

9 Not conceited, thus notable;

10 Not boastful, thus meritorious;

11 Not proud, thus lasting.

12 Because a Tao follower does not scramble for fame and wealth from others, nobody can compete with him or her.

13 Is the ancient saying that "Who makes compromise can reach agreement" a lie?

14 It indeed saves people from harm.

Chapter 23

1 Do not impose orders arbitrarily, yet let everything develop spontaneously:
2 So, violent wind cannot blow ceaselessly, and heavy rain cannot last forever.
3 Who makes them so?
4 The sky and the earth.
5 The rage of the sky and the earth cannot last long, let alone the arbitrary act of humankind?
6 So, whoever follows the Tao acts according to the Tao;
7 Whoever follows conscience acts according to conscience;
8 Whoever follows death acts according to death.
9 The Tao welcomes whoever acts according to the Tao;
10 Conscience welcomes whoever acts according to conscience;
11 Death welcomes whoever acts according to death.

Chapter 24

1 Nobody can stand on tiptoe for long or walk for long with long strides.
2 Whoever is showy is not wise;
3 Whoever is conceited is not notable;
4 Whoever is boastful is not meritorious;
5 Whoever is arrogant is not lasting.
6 According to the Tao, it is to say:
7 Unnecessary food and superfluous acts wants nobody.
8 So, a Tao follower will not do so.

Chapter 25

1 The Tao, existing before the sky and the earth, is only One:

2 She, independent and invariable, is called Mother Of all.

3 I do not know Her name, so I have to name Her as the Tao and call Her as infinite;

4 The boundary of the Tao is endless, extending far into the distance, and when you return to the starting point, you realize just how vast its boundaries truly are.

5 So, the Tao is great, the sky is great, the earth is great, and the humankind is great;

6 There are four great entities in the universe, yet humankind is the last of the four.

7 Humankind follows the earth, the earth follows the sky, the sky follows the Tao, and the Tao lets all live spontaneously.

Chapter 26

1 Steadiness is base of frivolity, and calmness is mastery of impetuosity.
2 Therefore, when a Tao follower embarks on an extended journey, he or she does not go out of a carriage covered with curtains;
3 Although there is tasty food and beautiful scenery on the way, he or she stays calm and undisturbed.
4 What comes if a monarch is frivolous and impetuous?
5 Frivolity makes the monarch lose his or her base, and impetuosity makes a monarch lose his or her mastery.

Chapter 27

1 Whoever is good at driving a cart does not leave ruts, whoever is good at arguing does not leave a flaw, and whoever is good at calculating does not use a counter;

2 Whoever is good at locking a door does not use a bar, yet nobody can open it;

3 Whoever is good at binding does not tie a knot, yet nobody can undo it.

4 Therefore, a Tao follower is always good at finding every person's strong point, so there is not a worthless person;

5 A Tao follower is always good at discovering everything' s good quality, so there is not a useless thing.

6 This is the subtle wisdom.

7 So, whoever is good at doing so is a teacher to whoever is not, and the latter is a warning to the former.

8 Whoever does not respect his or her teacher and value his or her warning, though thinking highly of him or herself, is the biggest fool.

9 This is the shrewdest truth.

Chapter 28

1 Would rather stay modest, as the gorge of the nation, than complacent;

2 As the gorge of the nation, he or she will not lose their achievements and return to babyish innocence.

3 Would rather stay unknown, as the valley of the nation, than notable;

4 As the valley of the nation, he or she will not diminish their achievements and return to purity.

5 Purity is the key to lead a nation, and a Tao follower, with the key, can lead a nation.

6 So, the system that makes people pure will never harm them.

Chapter 29

1 Whoever wishes for a country to be well-ruled by directing it arbitrarily, I am certain it is impossible:

2 A country is sacred and cannot be ruled by arbitrary direction and control.

3 Arbitrary direction inevitably leads to ruin, and arbitrary control inevitably leads to loss.

4 Therefore, a Tao follower does not direct a country arbitrarily, thus avoid ruin it;

5 He or she does not control a country arbitrarily, thus avoid loss it.

6 People's natures vary—some are fast, some are slow, some are sturdy, and some are frail, some are diligent, and some are idle.

7 Therefore, a Tao follower does not exhibit excess, obsession or extremes.

Chapter 30

1 If a Tao follower governs a country, he or she will refrain from flaunting military might, as retribution will swiftly come:

2 Wherever armies are stationed, an overgrowth of brambles follows;

3 Wherever great battles are fought, large famines follow.

4 Whoever is well-versed in the art of war aims for victory, yet does not dare to flaunt armed forces:

5 Not conceited in victory;

6 Not boastful in victory;

7 Not proud in victory;

8 The goal is victory;

9 Not showing off armed forces after victory.

10 Whoever is arrogant will decline, which goes against the Tao, and whoever goes against the Tao will perish in advance.

Chapter 31

1 Resorting to force is an unfortunate thing that nobody desires, so a Tao follower does not flaunt armed forces.

2 A monarch depends on the civil servants to his or her left in peacetime and on the military officers to his or her right in time of war.

3 Resorting to force is not an auspicious endeavor, it's not a decision any monarch should make, and maintaining a calm and low-key mind is always the ideal approach.

4 Do not praise victory, and whoever does so delights in killing;

5 Whoever takes pleasure in killing loses the support of the people.

6 Left stands for happiness, and right stands for sadness.

7 The vice-commander stands to the left of the chief commander, and the latter stands to the right of the former, symbolizing that war should be treated as a funeral rite.

8 Gravely attend a war because a mass of people are killed.

9 Treat the victory via the funeral rite.

Chapter 32

1 The Tao is always unknown and pure;
2 Though the Tao is unknown, She is dominated by nobody.
3 If a monarch follows the Tao, everything will keep in order spontaneously.
4 If hot and cold airs meet between the sky and the earth, it will rain spontaneously without anybody's command.
5 All have the name, which is also called as being, when they appear, so they should know enough is enough:
6 Knowing that means staying away from danger.
7 The Tao to all is what the sea is to the rivers.

Chapter 33

1 Whoever knows others is clever, and
whoever knows him or herself is wise;
2 Whoever wins others is competent, and
whoever wins him or herself is strong.
3 Whoever stays content is rich, and
whoever does not give up is ambitious;
4 Whoever conserves his or her roots is
permanent, and whoever has immortal
spirit is lasting.

Chapter 34

1 People always say to me, " The Tao does not seem as great."
2 She does not seem as great because She is;
3 If She seems, She is not worthy of mention at all!
4 She is infinite and omnipresent;
5 All rely on Her to exist, yet She never refuses;
6 All depend on Her to succeed, yet She never claims the credit for Herself.
7 She encompasses all yet does not dominate all, so She is unknown;
8 She is relied on by all yet does not impose arbitrary orders to all, so She is great.
9 It is because the Tao never boasts itself as great that the Tao is truly great.

Chapter 35

1 A Tao follower, whom people will follow;
2 If they do so, they will not get harmed,
  and live in peace and content.
3 Music and food can stop the passengers;
4 The Tao is flavorless, invisible and
  inaudible, yet Her effect never ever
  ceases.

Chapter 36

1 In order to close it, first open it;
2 In order to weaken it, first strengthen it;
3 In order to abolish it, first raise it;
4 In order to achieve it, first pay for it.
5 These are called subtle strategies.
6 Modesty and caution defeat stubbornness and conceit.
7 Fish cannot leave a deep pond, and a state's arsenal cannot be flaunted.

Chapter 37

1 The Tao, never acting arbitrarily, never fails.

2 If a monarch does not direct the country arbitrarily, people will become civilized spontaneously;

3 Civilization brings desires, and I will suppress desires with the purity of the Tao.

4 Suppress desires with Her purity, and then people stay content.

5 If they stay content and keep calm, the country will become righteous spontaneously.

Chapter 38

1 Whoever does not boast of his or her merits has merit;

2 Whoever boasts of his or her merits has no merit.

3 Whoever has merit does not act arbitrarily, and is selfless;

4 Whoever has no merit acts arbitrarily, and is selfish.

5 Whoever is not impartial acts arbitrarily, and is selfish;

6 Whoever is factious acts arbitrarily, and is selfish;

7 Whoever is privileged acts arbitrarily, and rolls up sleeves to erase his or her protesters.

8 So, after the Tao is abandoned, there comes boasting of merits;

9 After boasting of merits, there comes partiality;

10 After partiality, there comes faction;

11 After faction, there comes privileged system.

12 Privileged system, embodying the ruin of loyalty and honesty, is the source of trouble;

13 Fortune-telling, merely seeing the surface of the Tao, is the beginning of

stupidity.

14 Therefore, based on permanence, yet not on temporariness;

15 Based on reality, yet not on surface.

16 So, abandon temporariness and surface, but retain permanence and reality.

Chapter 39

1 The ancient Tao followers:
2 The sky was clear because of following the Tao;
3 The earth was quiet because of following the Tao;
4 Gods had lasting spirit because of following the Tao;
5 The canyon was full of water because of following the Tao;
6 All existed because of following the Tao;
7 A monarch was respected by people because of following the Tao;
8 That is to say:
9 The sky, losing clearness, would explode;
10 The earth, losing quiet, would collapse;
11 Gods, losing lasting spirit, would be abandoned;
12 The canyon, losing water, would dry up;
13 All, losing being, would be extinct;
14 A monarch, losing people' s respect, would leave office.
15 So, respect roots in modesty, and admiration bases on not scrambling for fame and wealth from people.
16 Therefore, a monarch called him or herself as unsuccessful, merciless or useless.

17 Was not it because he or she stay modest?
18 So, the highest praise does not come
   from arbitrary boast.
19 Therefore, I would rather constitute a
   hard stone than a sparking jade.

Chapter 40

1 Under the law of the Tao, all eventually returns to non-being.
2 The Tao lets all develop spontaneously, so nobody truly knows Her.
3 All root in being, and being roots in non-being.

Chapter 41

1 When the wise hear of the Tao, they strive to follow Her;

2 When the clever hear of the Tao, they half believe and half doubt Her;

3 When the foolish hear of the Tao, they laugh aloud at HER.

4 If the Tao is not laughed at, She is not worthy of mention at all.

5 So, the book of *Jian Yan* said:

6 "The Tao is bright but seems dim; the Tao is forward but seems backward; the Tao is flat but seems uneven.

7 "A successful person seems like a canyon; a learned person seems inadequate; a diligent person seems idle.

8 "A glorious thing seems humiliating; a pure thing seems flawed; a righteous thing seems hurtful.

9 "The most important things don't not need to get admitted by all; the loudest sound is soundless; the biggest shape is shapeless."

10 It is only the Tao who is unknown but good at helping and benefiting all.

Chapter 42

1 The Tao is only One; She gives rise to non-being and being; these two give rise to the sky, the earth and the humankind; these three give rise to everything.

2 Every thing is a unity of good and bad.

3 A monarch named him or herself unsuccessful, merciless and useless, but people will not name themselves so.

4 So, a person is either respected for modesty or despised for boast.

5 I will teach others what I was taught, too:

6 Whoever is stubborn and conceited does not meet a good end.

7 I will put this as the beginning of my teaching.

Chapter 43

1 The gentlest thing in the world can drive the firmest material.
2 She, shapeless, can go through the solid, so I know the good of not arbitrarily behaving.
3 Few people can grasp the good of not arbitrarily dictating and not arbitrarily behaving.

Chapter 44

1 Fame or life, which is more intimate?
2 Life or wealth, which is more important?
3 Possession of fame and wealth or loss of life, which is more dangerous?
4 Obsession incurs big expense, and voracity incurs large loss.
5 So, whoever is content does not make him or herself shameful, and whoever is temperate does not make him or herself dangerous, which is lasting.

Chapter 45

1 The Tao is intact but seems damaged, yet
Her effect will not stop;
2 The Tao is abundant but seems empty,
yet Her effect will not end.
3 What is straight seems curved, and
whoever is dexterous seems clumsy;
4 Whoever is eloquent seems stuttering,
and what is profitable seems unprofitable.
5 Calm defeats impulse, and composure
defeats impetuosity;
6 Purity and lack of desire make the
country just and strict.

Chapter 46

1 If a country follows the Tao, war horses are used to haul manure carts;
2 If a country neglects the Tao, war horses give birth on the battlefield.
3 The biggest disaster is insatiability, and the biggest sin is acquisitiveness;
4 So, whoever is content is content for ever.

Chapter 47

1 Need not go for a long journey, yet know a country' s condition;
2 Need not peep at celestial objects, yet see a country' s destiny;
3 The farther to go, the less to know about a country.
4 Therefore, a Tao follower does not go for a long journey, yet knows a country' s condition;
5 He or she does not peep at celestial objects, yet sees a country's destiny;
6 He or she does not act arbitrarily, yet gets success.

Chapter 48

1 If people follow worldly desires, their desire will increase;

2 If people follow the Tao, their desire will diminish.

3 It diminishes till they do not act arbitrarily any longer.

4 Whoever does not act arbitrarily will not fail.

5 Never interfere with a country arbitrarily:

6 Whoever interferes with the country arbitrarily has no right to govern it.

7 Therefore, a Tao follower does not value rare treasures, does not follow worldly desires, rectifies people's wrongs, lets everything develop spontaneously, but does not act arbitrarily.

Chapter 49

1 A Tao follower is always selfless and impartial.
2 I offer unconditional help to whoever unconditionally helps others;
3 I also do that to whoever does not;
4 Unconditional help is realized.
5 I keep my promise to whoever keeps his or her promise;
6 I also do that to whoever does not;
7 Promise is realized.
8 A Tao follower does not administer a country arbitrarily.
9 People focus on worldly desires, and a Tao follower lets them return to babyish purity.

Chapter 50

1 From the cradle to the grave:
2 A third of people lives a long life;
3 A third of people lives a short life;
4 A third of people could live a long life
   but fail to.
5 Why do they fail to?
6 Because they live in luxury.
7 It is said whoever is good at protecting
   his or her life does not run into a rhino or
   a tiger when walking on the land, and
   does not get hurt by the blade of weapon
   when joining the army.
8 The rhino has nowhere to strike its horn,
   the tiger has nowhere to use its claws, the
   weapon has nowhere to cast its blade.
9 What for?
10 Because he or she does not act arbitrarily,
   they will not court death.

Chapter 51

1 The Tao gives rise to all;
2 The achievement of the Tao raises them;
3 Humankind names them;
4 Environment distinguishes them.
5 Therefore, the Tao and the achievement of the Tao are revered by all.
6 They never impose arbitrary dictates, but rather allow for spontaneous development, thereby earning reverence.
7 So, the Tao gives rise to them, and the achievement of the Tao raises them, which lets them develop, produce and get secured.
8 She does not control them when they appear, does not depends on them when they develop, and does not dominates them when they succeed.
9 This is the greatest merit.

Chapter 52

1 All root in being, as the root of all.
2 Whoever knows the root of all knows all;
3 If knowing all, it is necessary to defend the root of all, which entails no danger throughout life.
4 Let people pure and leave the source arousing desire, so they are not in trouble all life long;
5 Let them crafty and have the source arousing desire, so they are out of cure all life long.
6 Whoever can stay careful is wise, and whoever can keep modest is strong;
7 Let people, with the light of wisdom, return to carefulness, and leave no trouble behind themselves.
8 This is called the subtle permanence.

Chapter 53

1 If I am a little wise, I will follow the Tao, and fear to go stray.
2 The Tao is righteous, but humankind is crooked:
3 The palace is so splendid;
4 The farmland is so wasted;
5 The granary is so empty;
6 They, in gaudy attires and with a sharp sward, are tired of sumptuous feasts, and grabbing superfluous wealth.
7 They are the chieftain of bandits, which is against the Tao.

Chapter 54

1 Whoever is persevering never abandons the Tao, and whoever is devout never betrays the Tao, so their posterity will not get extinct.

2 If a person follows the Tao, the person's achievement is real;

3 If a family follows the Tao, the family's achievement is adequate;

4 If a village follows the Tao, the village's achievement is lasting;

5 If a state follows the Tao, the state's achievement is rich;

6 If a nation follows the Tao, the nation's achievement is general.

7 So, when know a person's faith, know the person;

8 When know a family's faith, know the family;

9 When know a village's faith, know the village;

10 When know a state's faith, know the state;

11 When know a nation's faith, know the nation.

12 Why do I know the nation?

13 By this way.

Chapter 55

1 Whoever has a great achievement is like a new born baby:

2 Noxious insects do not sting it, fierce beasts do not hurt it, and big birds do not paw it;

3 It is weak but fists tightly, and never knows about consummation but often has an erection because it is energetic;

4 It cries aloud but does not get a hoarse throat because it is content.

5 Whoever is content has an immortal spirit, and whoever has an immortal spirit is wise;

6 Whoever lives in luxury is disastrous, and whoever is driven by desire is conceited.

7 Whoever is arrogant will decline, which goes against the Tao, and whoever goes against the Tao will perish in advance.

Chapter 56

1 Whoever does not issue arbitrary commands is wise, and whoever does so is unwise.

2 Let people pure and away from the source arousing desire;

3 Frustrate their pride, and stop their conflicts;

4 Fuse their intelligence, and normalize their customs.

5 This is called as the most profound harmony.

6 So, whoever is meritorious neither shows partiality for nor pushes aside others, neither profits him or herself nor harm others, and neither overestimate him or herself nor underestimate others.

7 So, he or she is respected by all.

Chapter 57

1 Administer a state with a fair and strict attitude, fight a war with unexpected tactics, and do not administer the state arbitrarily.

2 Why do I know it is so?

3 By these reasons below:

4 The more taboos are, the more destitute people are;

5 The more weapons are, the more turbulent a state is;

6 The more tricky people are, the more odd things are;

7 The more decrees are, the more robbers are.

8 So,when a Tao follower directs a state, he or she will say:

9 "I abide by law, and people are civilized spontaneously;

10 "I stay calm, and people are righteous spontaneously;

11 "I do not interfere arbitrarily, and people are affluent spontaneously;

12 "I am content, and people are pure spontaneously."

Chapter 58

1 If a monarch does not interfere arbitrarily, people are pure and upright;
2 If a monarch does so, people are tricky and cunning.
3 Good luck is escorted by bad, and the latter is accompanied by the former;
4 Who knows the final result?
5 There is no absolute answer.
6 Right can go wrong, and good can turn bad;
7 People have got confused about it for a long time.
8 Therefore, a Tao follower is righteous but not hurtful, decisive but not wayward, frank but not insolent, and intelligent but not showy.

Chapter 59

1 To govern the country in accordance with Heaven, nothing is more important than thrift:

2 Because, thrift is to prepare in advance;

3 Whoever prepares in advance is to continuously accumulate achievement;

4 Whoever continuously accumulates achievement has no invincible trouble;

5 Whoever has no invincible trouble has unfathomable power;

6 Whoever has unfathomable power is able to take the heavy responsibility to lead a state;

7 Whoever masters the essence to lead a state can stay long.

8 This is the everlasting truth of governing a country.

Chapter 60

1 Governing so big a state is like cooking such small shrimp and crabs, which are not flavoured arbitrarily.

2 If a country follows the Tao as the example, the wicked will disappear;

3 It does not mean that the wicked are extinct, but means that they can no longer deceive people.

4 Not only the wicked but also a Tao follower is unable to deceive people;

5 Both the wicked and a Tao follower are unable to deceive people, so the achievement belongs to people.

Chapter 61

1 A big state, like the sea, should stay in the lower reaches as the basis and centre of a country.

2 The modest always defeat the conceited because they stay lowly with calmness.

3 So, if a big state modestly treats a small state, the former is trusted by the latter;

4 If the latter modestly treats the former, the latter is trusted by the former.

5 So, either a big state with a lowly attitude is trusted by a small state, or the latter with a lowly attitude is trusted by the former.

6 A big state just wants to lead a small state, and the latter just wants to rely on the former.

7 Thus both of them can reach their aims, and it is good for a big state to stay modest.

Chapter 62

1 The Tao, the origin of all mysteries, is the treasure of whoever offers unconditional help;

2 It is good for whoever does not offer unconditional help to retain Her.

3 Good words can win people' s respect, and good deeds can win people' s admiration;

4 Even if a person does not offer unconditional help, does he or she have any reasons to forsake that truth?

5 So, when a monarch ascends the throne, and subjects assume office, it is better to present that truth than to celebrate it.

6 Why did the ancient value that truth?

7 Did not they say that they could gain help in need and pardon after making a mistake because of it?

8 So, that truth was valued.

Chapter 63

1 No flavouring food arbitrarily, no interfering arbitrarily, and no behaving arbitrarily.

2 Big grows from small, and much comes from little;

3 Solve difficult things when they are easy, address big issues when they are small.

4 Difficult things must be easy at the beginning, big issues must be small at the beginning;

5 Therefore, a Tao follower will not wait to address issues until they become big, so it makes him or her great.

6 Whoever easily promises can rarely keep his or her words, and whoever underestimates a difficulty will meet more difficulties;

7 Therefore, a Tao follower does not underestimate a difficulty, so he or she has no difficulty.

Chapter 64

1 When the situation is not turbulent, it is easy to control;

2 When the situation is not obvious, it is easy to scheme;

3 When the situation is not severe, it is easy to deal with;

4 When the situation is not big, it is easy to resolve.

5 The crisis should be dealt with before it appears, and the chaos should be managed before it erupts.

6 The great tree is born from a tiny sprout;

7 The nine-story high platform rises from the lowest level;

8 The long journey starts from the starting step.

9 People always fail when they nearly make it;

10 If they can carefully treat it at both the beginning and end, they will not lose.

Chapter 65

1 Ancient Tao followers did not teach
  people crafty, but taught them pure:
2 People are difficult to lead because they
  are tricky.
3 So, rule by man is disastrous to a state;
4 Rule by law is fortunate to it.
5 When understand the distinction between
  them, understand how to lead a state.
6 Never quitting rule by law is the biggest
  achievement.
7 Rule by law has a profound influence and
  helps people return to purity, and then
  makes a nation in order.

Chapter 66

1 The sea is the king of all rivers because it stays below them.
2 So it is the king of them.
3 Therefore, if a Tao follower wants to lead a country, he or she must keep his or her words modest;
4 If he or she wants to govern a country, he or she must put people' s interests in front of his or hers.
5 Therefore, if a Tao follower leads a country, people do not feel burdened;
6 If he or she governs a country, people' s interests are not harmed.
7 Therefore, people all support yet do not hate him or her.
8 It is because he or she does not scramble for fame and wealth from others that nobody is able to compete with him or her.

Chapter 67

1 I have three pieces of treasures, which I retain and guard:
2 The first is selflessness; the second is thrift; the third is not scrambling for profit from people.
3 Whoever stays selfless can be brave;
4 Whoever stays thrifty can exist long;
5 Whoever does not scramble for profit from people can lead a country.
6 But now, whoever stays selfish wants to become brave;
7 Whoever lives in luxury wants to exist long;
8 Whoever scrambles for profit from people wants to lead a country.
9 Impossible!
10 Selflessness will make attack triumphant and defense firm.
11 Providence will arm with selflessness whoever She wants to save.

Chapter 68

1 Whoever is good at commanding troops does not flaunt force;

2 Whoever is good at fighting does not lose his or her temper;

3 Whoever is good at winning a war does not confront the tough with toughness;

4 Whoever is good at making proper use of personnel does not stay conceited.

5 These achievements are not obtained by pride and conceit, which accords with the Tao.

6 It was the most brilliant strategy in the ancient times.

Chapter 69

1 Whoever is good at directing troops said,
  "I dare not attack but defend, and dare
  not invade an inch but retreat a foot."

2 It is unnecessary to array the troop, to
  roll sleeves, to kill an enemy, and to
  abuse weapons.

3 Nothing is more disastrous than
  underestimating the enemy, which almost
  makes my three treasures ruined;

4 So, when two equally matched armies
  confront each other in a battle, the
  solemn one wins.

Chapter 70

1 My words are easy to understand and to follow;
2 Yet people are unable to understand and to follow.
3 The theme of what I say is visible, and the subject of what I do is knowable.
4 People are proud and stubborn, so they are unable to understand me.
5 Few can understand me, and fewer can follow my words.
6 Therefore, a Tao follower is wearing coarse clothes, a jade under the bosom.

Chapter 71

1 Knowing that you are not wise is good;
2 Not knowing about it is a disaster.
3 A Tao follower has no disaster, because
   he or she knows what a disaster is.
4 It is because a Tao follower knows what
   a disaster is that he or she has no disaster.

Chapter 72

1 If people no longer fear the menace from above, a big chaos will come from below.
2 Do not arbitrarily occupy people's homes, and do not arbitrarily squeeze people's lives;
3 It is because their livings are not exploited that they do not feel resentful.
4 Therefore, a Tao follower is wise yet not showy, and self-respecting yet not arrogant.
5 So, abandon flaunt and arrogance yet retain wisdom and self-respect.

Chapter 73

1 Whoever is courageous confronts death
with composure, and whoever is
cowardly cling to their final breath of life.
2 Either comprises a good side and a bad,
and who knows whom Providence
dislikes?
3 She does not pursue fame and wealth, but
achieves success; she does not dictate,
but responds; she does not call forth, but
arrives - deliberate and adept in planning.
4 The network of opportunity is vast and
imperceptible, yet nothing escapes its
grasp.

Chapter 74

1 If people no longer fear death, does it matter to threaten them with death?
2 If they always fear death and then I catch and execute whoever does evil, who dares to do evil again?
3 There are always judges who pronounce death sentences, and taking the place of a judge to pronounce a death sentence is like replacing a carpenter to whittle a wood.
4 Rarely does whoever replaces a carpenter to whittle wood not cut his or her own hand.

Chapter 75

1 It is because a monarch levies taxes
   excessively that people live in hunger
   and poverty.
2 Therefore, they are in hunger and poverty.
3 It is because a country is under rule by
   man that people are difficult to lead.
4 Therefore, they are difficult to lead.
5 It is because a monarch lives in luxury
   that people risk their lives to revolt.
6 Therefore, they risk their lives to revolt.
7 Whoever is not obsessive about worldly
   desires is wiser than whoever is.

Chapter 76

1 A living body is supple, yet a dead one is stiff;
2 A living twig is tender, yet a withered one is brittle.
3 So, conceit and stubbornness belong to stiffness;
4 Modesty and prudence belong to suppleness.
5 Therefore, whoever is conceited about military forces is as weak as a withered twig.
6 Conceit is in a disadvantageous position, and modesty is in an advantageous one.

Chapter 77

1 The deed of the Tao is like the archery:
2 Make the bow lower if it is too high, and make it higher if it is too low;
3 Make it looser if it is too tight, and make it tighter if it is too loose.
4 The Tao decreases superfluity to increase deficiency.
5 Humankind, contrarily, decreases deficiency to increase superfluity.
6 Who can decrease superfluity to increase deficiency for a country?
7 Only a Tao follower!
8 Therefore, a Tao follower does not depend on things when they develop, and does not claim credit for it when things succeed.
9 He or she does not want to show off his or her merits.

Chapter 78

1 Although water is softer than others, it is more effective than others to penetrate a firm thing because its characteristic is unique.

2 Prudence defeats stubbornness, and modesty wins conceit;

3 Nobody does not know, but nobody can do it.

4 Therefore, a Tao follower believes:

5 "Whoever bears the shame of the state is called the head of it, and whoever bears the disaster of the state is called the leader of it."

6 Truth sounds ironic.

Chapter 79

1 When a conflict is reconciled, there must be a resentment left behind.

2 So how can it be said that the conflict is completely resolved?

3 So a conflict should be reconciled in conscience.

4 Therefore, the Tao follower abides by the contract and does not arbitrarily press the other party.

5 Whoever has a conscience fulfills the contract, and whoever does not have a conscience presses for the immediate payment of debts.

6 The Tao is always good at giving to humankind.

Chapter 80

1 Do not covet lands and population of other countries.

2 Do not let people overly depend on various instruments and risk their lives to flee away.

3 Although there are boats and carts, it is unnecessary for people to flee away by them;

4 Although there are soldiers, it is unnecessary to array them to threaten people.

5 Let people return to the purity of ancient times:

6 Content with their food; content with their clothes; content with their dwellings; content with their customs.

7 Peoples, in the neighbouring states, can see each other and hear dogs barking and cocks crowing from each other, yet it is unnecessary to flee to each other's state in time of hardship or danger.

Chapter 81

1 Not all true words are pleasant, and not all pleasant words are true;

2 Not all selfless people are publicized, not all publicized people are selfless;

3 Not all wise people are learned, and not all learned people are wise.

4 A Tao follower does not hoard for him or herself, and tries his or her best to help others, yet becomes more wealthy;

5 He or she tries his or her best to give to others, yet becomes more sufficient.

6 The Tao benefits yet does not harm all;

7 The Tao follower helps yet does not scramble for fame and wealth from others.